# KINGFISHER FAMILY, TELL US YOUR STORY.

## BY RICHARD ARNOLD
## PUBLISHED 2024

ISBN 978-0-6451296-0-1

PHOTO CREDITS: ALL PHOTOS WERE TAKEN BY THE AUTHOR EXCEPT:

- THE BUFF-BREASTED PARADISE KINGFISHER WAS TAKEN BY DAVID MEAD (USED WITH PERMISSION)
- THE IMAGE OF COSMIC CLIFFS IN THE CARINA NEBULA ON THE FRONT COVER, THIS PAGE AND BACK COVER WAS PRODUCED BY NASA AND THE SPACE TELESCOPE SCIENCE INSTITUTE (STSCI) FROM NASA'S JAMES WEBB SPACE TELESCOPE

# Introduction

In this book, the Kingfisher Family tells their story of how they have emerged in relationship with all life since the journey of the Universe began over 13.7 billion years ago.

The 10 members of the Kingfisher Family in Australia, each tell part of the family story as well as their own individual story.

Collectively, they explain how interdependent and inter-related they are with other beings, including humans. They particularly mention the challenges to their unique ecological niche due to the actions of human beings.

They call on humans to respect their right to exist and thrive.

# The Kingfisher Story

Like you humans, we have evolved from the flaring forth of a Wave of Love from our Loving Source over 13.7 billion years ago.

The resulting Universe became a living being evoking all the unique expressions of creation like plants, fish, animals, and us – the birds of the world.

How did this come about?
Shortly after the flaring forth, the Universe created hydrogen atoms which gathered into clouds and formed galaxies.

Galaxies then formed stars and planets.

# Azure Kingfisher

*I live by rivers, creeks, swamps, and lakes, often hiding in overhanging vegetation. I am not always easy to see as I hide, waiting to pick up a small fish or a yabby. When humans pollute the water and kill my food sources, dam rivers, clear vegetation around lakes and creeks, or empty my wetland homes, my future is threatened. You humans need to understand my home, and my role in the ecosystem and respect my right to play my part in the journey of the Universe.*

The Earth formed some 4.6 billion years ago, and the first signs of life appeared after some 3.5 billion years.

Creatures began to live on the land around 400 million years ago and our ancestors, the birds, probably first appeared around 150 million years ago.

In more recent times, our family has evolved into 119 species, with 10 of our family living in Australia. Our ancestors slowly worked with Mother Earth to find new ways of thriving and inter-relating with all other beings – just like you humans.

# Laughing Kookaburra

*I am a woodland bird. I like to perch in trees and survey the surrounding area looking for a lizard or snake to eat. When humans clear my woodland home, my supermarket disappears as well as my nesting places. The new threat of climate change is very real for me – more frequent and intense bushfires are destroying my home and the future home of my descendants.*

The Kingfisher family now appears in many forms – each of us prefers different habitats, but we have always been prepared to adapt, change, and become a more vital, diverse, and crucial presence within our interdependent Earth, as we seek a deeper participation in the journey of the Universe.

From hydrogen atoms to incredibly formed and coloured beings, we have emerged here on Mother Earth.

We have been created by the Universe and given gifts so that we can give back to the Universe just like you humans. Our gifts help to maintain the delicate balance of Mother Earth in wetlands, forests, and arid lands – contributing to the interdependence of all beings.

# Blue-winged Kookaburra

Like my cousin the Laughing Kookaburra, I too like living in open woodland. My major difference is that I love the warmer weather, so my preference is to live in more Northern parts of Australia. Again, the threat of forest clearing, and dangerous bushfires aggravated by climate change, threaten my future.

Notice our colours which help us blend into the environment, making it easier for us to hunt and avoid being hunted. They also help us find a mate and create new kingfishers. They are a glorious gift from our Loving Source.

We can continue to be a wonderful presence on Mother Earth, and praise our Loving Source. But we need the home in which we have evolved over countless generations – a home in which habitat changes have been gradual and harmonious.

However, you humans seem hell-bent on destroying our home because you only think about what is of value to you - your own comforts, power, and security.

# Torresian Kingfisher

*I love hanging out in tidal mangrove areas. From a small, perched tree, I can see small crustaceans and fish – I swoop down on them and gobble them down.*

*Overheating due to climate change is causing the destruction of some mangrove species and affecting my homeland. We are also not immune from fires and floods – extreme weather events which are also aggravated by climate change.*

Our Loving Source cares for all beings! Humans, widen your vision; lift your eyes beyond yourself; understand that you are just part of a much bigger story in which you and we and the whole cosmos are involved.

Let me speak on behalf of my Kingfisher family: We and our offspring have our integrity, habitat, and purpose. We are each called to live our lives in our specific places and unique ways and honour our Loving Source.

We are part of "wild" Mother Earth for which our Loving Source cares deeply.

# Red-backed Kingfisher

I am a dry country bird, often living far from water in semi-arid woodland. I eat small mammals, insects, and reptiles. Climate change is causing more frequent and prolonged droughts and even for me it is becoming a challenge to eke out an existence. You humans have also introduced many pests, in particular cats, and these also threaten my existence.

Slow down, stop and listen to us. Stop and open your eyes and see us – look at our wonderful ways of hunting, of building shelter, and our amazing colours.

Your human self-absorption threatens all our family, all life on Mother Earth which has evolved over billions of years.

Take time out to be still and silent. Allow yourselves to connect with the Wave of Love that courses through the Universe. You will become energised with a power that is gentle and clear-sighted.

# Yellow-billed Kingfisher

*I live in tropical and monsoon rainforests. I blend into my environment and search for insects and reptiles on the edges of the forest. My home can often be damaged by severe weather events such as cyclones – and these are becoming more intense with climate change.*

You will reconnect with Mother Earth and become part of the bigger story. This will give you the "courage to be", to "give life a go" in a spirit of love and joy.

Imagine yourselves as partners with the Universe on its evolving journey.
The Universe gives us each unique gifts which we can give back and enhance the Universe.

We each have a short time to play our unique part on this journey and be part of the collective history of the Universe.

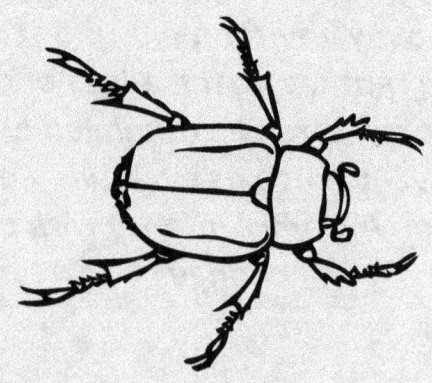

# Little Kingfisher

*I am one of the smallest kingfishers. I sit quietly beside rivers, creeks, mangroves, and wetlands, waiting to dive down on small fish and insects. With more extreme weather events resulting from climate change, my homelands may become raging torrents or dry up completely.*

You humans have several great teachers who can help you change your attitude toward Mother Earth and my Kingfisher family.

There was a human called Jesus who cared for the vulnerable, the outsider, and spoke truth to power in a non-violent manner.

Following his way may help you gain the courage to connect with the Wave of Love which courses through the Universe. Then you might engage with the Universe in reverence, wonder, and thanksgiving. And when you love something, you will not bear to harm it.

# Sacred Kingfisher

*I am quite a well-known member of my family in Australia. I migrate from the Northern parts to the South of the country in summer. I prefer open woodland for my home where I hunt insects and reptiles for food. The big threat to my home is the increasing intensity and regularity of forest fires – aggravated by human-induced climate change.*

You might wait with joyful hope that new possibilities for wholeness, awareness, creativity, and fulfillment are ahead and about to break into the present.

I hope that you are becoming aware that each of us – plants, trees, birds, animals, humans – has evolved with the Universe and so we will always belong to it.

We can all give thanks that through connecting with the waves of love and re-radiating this love, and through sharing our unique gifts and passion for life we become the Universe, intimately bonded with it for eternity.

# Buff Breasted Paradise Kingfisher

I visit Australia from New Guinea each year during the summer where I live in the rainforest. Here I look for a termite mound on the forest floor to use as a nest. I am not easy to spot in the forest as I stay very still waiting for my prey. However, you can recognise me by my long tail, particularly when I fly. Land clearing is a big threat to my existence, since without a termite mound, I cannot breed.

Come and join with my Kingfisher family, as we all participate in the unfolding journey of the Universe together.

# Forest Kingfisher

*I live in warm forest areas, and I like to be close to water. You can often see me perched on tree branches or power lines. From these vantage points I locate my prey and dive down to seize it. Like my cousins, land clearing and forest fires are big threats to my existence, and these are becoming more frequent and intense due to climate change.*

www.ingramcontent.com/pod-product-compliance
Lightning Source LLC
Chambersburg PA
CBHW071848290426
44109CB00017B/1969